MILOS

Travel Guide

2025

A Detailed Guide to the Best-Kept Secrets, Best Beaches, Boat Tours & Spectacular Must-See Spots & Unforgettable Escape in Greece Island

Robert I. Manley

Copyright

Table of Content

Forward

Welcome to Milos, a captivating island that invites you to step off the beaten path and into a world of breathtaking beauty, rich history, and unforgettable experiences. Whether you're drawn to its dramatic landscapes, crystal-clear waters, or the charm of its ancient villages, Milos offers something truly special for every traveler. As you hold this guide in your hands, I want you to feel the excitement of embarking on an adventure that promises to be unlike any other.

Milos is a place where time slows down, allowing you to truly immerse yourself in its natural wonders. From the moon-like white cliffs of Sarakiniko Beach to the pirate hideaway of Kleftiko, this island is a playground for those seeking both relaxation and exploration. Its unspoiled beaches, hidden coves, and traditional fishing villages offer the kind of serenity and authenticity that many islands in the Cyclades have lost over time.

But Milos is more than just its stunning landscapes. It's a land steeped in history and culture. The ancient ruins, the sacred catacombs, and the iconic Venus de Milo – all of these tell the story of a rich past that has shaped the present-day island. Whether you're a history buff, a nature lover, or someone simply seeking a peaceful getaway, Milos is an island that promises to captivate your heart.

This guide is designed to be your trusted companion on your journey through Milos. It will take you through the must-see attractions, the hidden gems, and the authentic experiences that make this island one of Greece's best-kept secrets. Whether you're planning a quick getaway or an extended stay, you'll find detailed itineraries, practical tips, and insider knowledge to help you make the most of your time on the island.

As you read these pages, I encourage you to embrace the spirit of adventure. Step into the unknown, discover new sights, and connect with the local culture. Milos is waiting for you with open arms, ready to offer you an unforgettable escape. Your journey to this magical island starts here. Let this guide be the key that unlocks the beauty and wonder of Milos for you.

Welcome To Milos

Close your eyes for a moment and imagine this: the sun dips low over the Aegean, casting a golden glow over rugged cliffs and sapphire waters. The salty breeze dances through your hair as you step onto the powdery sands of a secluded cove, waves lapping gently at the shore. The scent of freshly grilled seafood wafts through the air from a nearby taverna, where locals laugh and toast to another perfect evening. **This is Milos—the Cycladic island that captures the soul and refuses to let go.**

I have traveled to many places, but there is something truly **magnetic** about Milos. It's not just the **dazzling turquoise waters** or the **jaw-dropping volcanic landscapes**, though they certainly help. It's the **feeling**—that rare blend of tranquility and adventure, of authenticity and discovery. Here, time slows down, and every corner whispers a story, from the ancient catacombs to the dramatic sea caves carved by centuries of wind and waves.

If you're looking for **an island that surprises, delights, and enchants at every turn**, then you're in the right place.

Welcome to Milos—**the Cycladic gem that will steal your heart**.

Why Visit Milos in 2025?

Milos has always been breathtaking, but in 2025, it offers something **even more special**. Unlike its bustling neighbors, Santorini and Mykonos, Milos remains **charmingly authentic**, a place where you can experience Greece **as it was meant to be**—raw, unspoiled, and effortlessly beautiful.

Here's why 2025 is the perfect time to visit:

1. Fewer Crowds, More Magic

Milos has been gaining popularity, but it still **remains blissfully uncrowded compared to Santorini and Mykonos**. Even in peak season, you'll find **hidden beaches, quiet tavernas, and peaceful sunsets** without jostling for space.

2. Sustainability Efforts & Eco-Friendly Travel

In 2025, Milos continues its **push toward sustainable tourism**. Many hotels now use solar energy, **local farms** supply tavernas with fresh ingredients, and new **eco-conscious boat tours** allow visitors to explore with minimal impact on the environment. If you love nature and want to travel responsibly, this is **the place to do it**.

3. Perfect Weather for Every Traveler

Whether you visit in the warmth of summer (June–August) or the mild, golden autumn (September–October), **Milos never disappoints**. Even in the spring months (April–May), the island blooms with **wildflowers and quiet beaches**, offering an intimate escape.

4. Unbeatable Natural Beauty

There's a reason Milos **frequently tops lists of the most beautiful Greek islands**. From **the lunar-like landscapes of Sarakiniko** to the **secluded paradise of Tsigrado Beach**, this island is a **living postcard**.

5. A Haven for Food Lovers

Milos is a dream for **foodies**. Fresh seafood, creamy local cheeses, and the island's famous **ladenia (Greek-style pizza with tomatoes and onions)** make dining here an experience in itself.

Simply put, Milos in 2025 is **the dream destination**—whether you're an adventurer, a couple seeking romance, a solo traveler looking for serenity, or a history lover eager to uncover secrets of the past.

A Brief History of Milos

Milos isn't just beautiful—it's **steeped in history**. Long before it became a traveler's paradise, it was a **hub of ancient civilizations, a battleground for empires, and a home to artists, miners, and seafarers**.

1. The Birthplace of the Venus de Milo

One of the world's most **famous sculptures**, the **Venus de Milo**, was discovered here in 1820. Now housed in the **Louvre Museum in Paris**, this masterpiece is a testament to the island's artistic legacy.

2. A Crossroads of Ancient Civilizations

Milos' **strategic location** made it highly valuable to the **Minoans, Mycenaeans, and later, the Athenians and Romans**. The island's rich deposits of **obsidian**, a volcanic glass used for tools and weapons, fueled its economy and put Milos on the map as an important trade center.

3. The Early Christian Catacombs

One of Greece's most significant **Christian sites**, the **Catacombs of Milos**, dates back to the 1st century AD. Used as underground burial chambers and places of worship, they are a chilling yet fascinating reminder of the island's deep religious roots.

4. The Ottoman Era and Modern Times

Milos saw **centuries of change**, from the **Venetians to the Ottomans**. Today, it thrives as a blend of **traditional Greek**

charm and modern tourism, welcoming visitors to experience its **timeless beauty**.

With every step you take in Milos, **you're walking through history**—whether you're exploring ancient ruins, wandering through old fishing villages, or simply watching the sunset over the Aegean.

What Makes Milos Unique?

What sets Milos apart from **other Greek islands**? Why do travelers who come here **fall deeply in love and vow to return**? Let me tell you.

1. The Most Stunning & Diverse Beaches in Greece

If you think you've seen **beautiful beaches**, Milos will **redefine your expectations**. The island boasts **over 70 beaches**, each with its **own personality**.

- **Sarakiniko**: A white, moon-like landscape that feels like another planet.
- **Kleftiko**: A pirate's hideout, accessible only by boat, with **dramatic sea caves** and crystal-clear waters.

- **Tsigrado**: A secret cove, reached by a rope-and-ladder descent, perfect for the adventurous.

2. A Volcanic Wonderland

Milos is **not just an island—it's a geological masterpiece**. The **volcanic origin** has given the island an incredible variety of **rock formations, sea caves, and mineral deposits**, creating landscapes that **don't exist anywhere else in Greece**.

3. A True Hidden Gem

Unlike its famous Cycladic siblings, **Milos remains delightfully authentic**. Here, **locals still greet you warmly, tavernas serve homemade dishes with love, and life moves at a blissful, unhurried pace.**

4. An Adventurer's Paradise

From **hiking along rugged coastal trails** to **snorkeling in hidden sea caves**, Milos is **a playground for explorers**. If you love nature, water, and adventure, **this island was made for you**.

5. A Place Where Time Slows Down

In Milos, you'll **wake up to the sound of waves, spend days discovering hidden treasures, and end your evenings watching sunsets that feel almost spiritual**. It's the kind of place where you truly **disconnect and reconnect—with nature, with history, and with yourself**.

How This Guide Will Help You

I know planning a trip can feel **overwhelming**—especially when you want to make **the most of every moment**. That's where this guide comes in.

What You'll Get from This Book:

✔ **Detailed itineraries** for all types of travelers
✔ **Insider tips** on the best restaurants, hotels, and activities
✔ **Hidden gems** most tourists never find
✔ **Practical advice** on getting around, costs, and must-knows
✔ **Cultural insights** so you can experience Milos like a local

Milos isn't just a destination—it's **an experience, a feeling, a love affair waiting to happen**. I'm here to make sure that when you step onto this island, **you see it in its fullest, most breathtaking light**.

Are you ready for the adventure of a lifetime?

Welcome to Milos. **Your journey starts now.**

Planning Your Trip to Milos

Planning a trip to Milos should feel exciting, not overwhelming. I know firsthand how many questions come up—**when to go, how to get there, how much to budget, and how to get around once you arrive**. The good news? Milos is one of those destinations where things **fall into place beautifully** with just a little preparation.

By the time you finish this section, you'll feel **fully prepared and reassured**, knowing exactly what to expect and how to make the most of your trip.

Best Time to Visit: Seasons & Weather

Milos is a year-round destination, but **when you visit it will shape your experience**. Some travelers prefer the **lively atmosphere of summer**, while others seek the **peaceful charm of the off-season**.

Spring (April–June): A Blossoming Paradise

Spring in Milos is **one of my personal favorites**. The island **awakens from winter with mild temperatures (18–25°C / 64–77°F), blooming wildflowers, and quiet beaches**. It's the perfect time for:

- **Hiking & exploring** the island's rugged landscapes.
- **Enjoying mild weather** without the summer crowds.
- **Getting better prices** on accommodation and flights.

If you love **a balance of warm weather and tranquility, May and early June are perfect**.

Summer (July–August): Peak Season & Beach Bliss

If your dream is **long beach days and lively island vibes**, summer is the time to come. Expect:

- **Hot, sunny weather (26–33°C / 79–91°F)**—perfect for swimming.
- **Buzzing nightlife and full restaurants** in Adamas and Plaka.
- **Higher prices and more visitors**, especially in August.

A tip from experience? **If you visit in summer, book your ferry, accommodation, and car rental well in advance.**

Autumn (September–October): The Sweet Spot

September and early October might just be **the best-kept secret** for visiting Milos. Why?

- **The sea is still warm** from summer, making swimming incredible.
- **The crowds thin out**, but businesses remain open.
- **The sunsets feel extra magical**, with crisp, clear skies.

This is my **top recommendation** if you want perfect beach days **without the high-season chaos**.

Winter (November–March): Quiet & Authentic

Milos in winter is **a different kind of beauty**—quiet, local, and deeply authentic. While it's **too cold for swimming (10–18°C / 50–64°F),** you can still:

- **Explore ancient sites and villages without crowds.**
- **Experience Milos like a local,** with cozy tavernas and quiet streets.
- **Find unbeatable accommodation deals.**

If you don't mind cooler temperatures and want a **slow, peaceful escape**, winter could be for you.

Best Time for Your Trip?

- **For adventure & sightseeing: May–June or September–October.**
- **For beach lovers & nightlife: July–August.**
- **For budget-friendly travel: April, early June, or late September.**
- **For a quiet retreat: November–March.**

How to Get to Milos: Flights & Ferries

Milos is **an island**, which means **you'll need to arrive by ferry or flight**. The right choice depends on **your budget, schedule, and where you're coming from.**

Flights to Milos

Milos has a **small but convenient airport (MLO),** mainly serving domestic flights from Athens.

- **Direct flights from Athens (ATH) take just 40 minutes.**
- **During summer, more flights are available**—book in advance!
- **No international flights yet**, so you'll need a layover in Athens.

Flying is **the fastest** way to reach Milos, but **seats fill up quickly in summer**, so I recommend booking **at least two months in advance**.

Ferries to Milos

Ferries offer **a scenic, budget-friendly alternative**, and honestly, they're part of the fun.

- **From Athens (Piraeus Port):**
    - **High-speed ferry**: ~3-4 hours (€50–€80).
    - **Regular ferry**: ~6-7 hours (€35–€60).

- **From Santorini, Mykonos, or Crete:** ~2-5 hours, depending on the route.

If you're already **island-hopping in Greece, ferries are the best way to travel**. Just book early in summer, as **seats sell out quickly**.

My Tip: If you get seasick, **opt for a high-speed ferry**—less time on the water means less chance of nausea!

Getting Around Milos: Transport Options & Tips

Once you arrive, you'll want to **explore freely**. Luckily, Milos has several great transport options.

1. Renting a Car: The Best Choice for Exploring

Milos is **best explored with a car**—especially if you want to reach **hidden beaches like Tsigrado or Firiplaka**.

- **Daily rental cost:** ~€40–€80 in summer, lower in the off-season.

- **Need an international driving permit?** If you're from outside the EU, yes.
- **Book in advance in summer**—rental cars sell out fast!

2. Scooters & ATVs: For Adventurers

If you're **comfortable on two wheels**, a **scooter or ATV** offers a **fun, flexible way to explore**.

- **Scooter rental:** ~€25–€40 per day.
- **ATV rental:** ~€40–€70 per day.
- **Only recommended if you have experience driving them.**

3. Public Transport: Budget-Friendly but Limited

Buses in Milos are **affordable (€2–€3 per ride) and reliable**, but they don't reach every beach. They mainly connect **Adamas, Plaka, Pollonia, and some beaches**.

- **Good for budget travelers**, but **not ideal for full island exploration.**

4. Taxis & Private Transfers: Expensive but Convenient

Taxis in Milos **aren't as common** as in big cities, and they can be pricey. If you rely on taxis, expect to pay **€15–€40 per ride**, depending on the distance.

Budgeting for Your Trip: Costs & Money-Saving Strategies

I know budgeting is important, so let's break down **what to expect**.

Average Daily Costs:

- **Budget traveler:** €50–€80 per day.
- **Mid-range traveler:** €100–€180 per day.
- **Luxury traveler:** €200+ per day.

Money-Saving Tips:

- **Visit in May, June, or September** for lower prices.
- **Stay in family-run guesthouses** instead of high-end hotels.
- **Use buses when possible** to save on car rentals.
- **Eat at local tavernas**—the best food is often the most affordable!

Essential Travel Documents & Requirements

Before you go, make sure you **have everything you need**.

1. Passport & Visa Requirements

- **EU citizens:** No visa needed.
- **US, Canada, UK, Australia:** No visa needed for stays under 90 days.
- **Other nationalities:** Check visa requirements online.

2. Travel Insurance: A Must-Have

I **always** recommend travel insurance. It **covers medical emergencies, trip cancellations, and lost luggage—worth every penny** for peace of mind.

3. Currency & Payment Methods

- **Currency:** Euro (€).
- **Credit cards are widely accepted**, but always carry some cash for **small villages and beach tavernas**.

Final Thoughts: Feel Confident About Your Trip!

Milos is one of the **easiest and most rewarding islands to visit**—but a little planning goes a long way. Now that you know **when to go, how to get there, how to get around, and how to budget**, you can **book your trip with confidence**.

Trust me—you're in for an **incredible adventure. Let's get ready to explore!**

Where to Stay in Milos

Choosing where to stay in Milos is just as exciting as planning what to do. Unlike some Greek islands where accommodations feel similar from one town to the next, Milos offers **distinct and diverse areas**, each with its own character, atmosphere, and charm. Whether you're looking for a **bustling port town**, a **romantic hilltop village**, or a **secluded hideaway by the sea**, there's a perfect place for you.

I've explored every corner of this island, and I can tell you that where you stay **shapes your experience**. Do you want to wake up to **calm sea views**, step outside into **lively tavernas**, or fall asleep in a **restored fisherman's house on the water's edge**? Let's dive into the **best areas to stay, the top accommodations, and unique stays** that will make your time in Milos unforgettable.

Best Areas to Stay: Adamas, Plaka, Pollonia & Beyond

Each part of Milos has its own distinct **energy and personality**. Some places are perfect for **first-time visitors**, while others are ideal for those looking for **seclusion, adventure, or romance**.

1. Adamas – The Heart of Convenience & Accessibility

If you want **the perfect mix of comfort, accessibility, and vibrant nightlife**, Adamas is the best place to stay. As the **main port of Milos**, it's where ferries arrive, where you'll find plenty of shops, restaurants, and where many boat tours start.

Why Stay Here?

- **Perfect for first-time visitors** who want an easy base to explore.
- **Great for nightlife and dining**, with tavernas and cocktail bars along the waterfront.
- **Close to public transport and car rentals**, making it easy to explore the island.
- **Many affordable stays**, from budget hotels to stylish boutique apartments.

Recommended Stays in Adamas:

- **Budget: Hotel Eleni** – A cozy, family-run spot just a short walk from the port.

- **Mid-range: Santa Maria Village** – A charming hotel with a pool and sea views.
- **Luxury: Milos Cove** – A high-end resort with breathtaking infinity pools.

2. Plaka – A Romantic Hilltop Retreat

Plaka is **Milos' most picturesque village**, perched high above the sea with **unbeatable sunset views**. If you love **charming alleys, whitewashed buildings, and a romantic atmosphere**, this is where you want to be.

Why Stay Here?

- **Perfect for couples and photographers** looking for postcard-perfect views.
- **Rich in history and culture**, with museums, churches, and traditional tavernas.
- **Unforgettable sunsets**, rivaling even Santorini.

Recommended Stays in Plaka:

- **Budget: Halara Studios** – Affordable and close to the best sunset spots.
- **Mid-range: Plaka Suites** – Chic apartments with private terraces.

- **Luxury: Villa Lord House** – A stunning 19th-century house with a breathtaking view.

3. Pollonia – A Tranquil Seaside Escape

Pollonia is **a peaceful fishing village** on the northeastern tip of Milos. If you want a **quiet, relaxing stay by the sea**, with **fresh seafood and beautiful swimming spots**, Pollonia is perfect.

Why Stay Here?

- **Ideal for families and couples** looking for a relaxed atmosphere.
- **Great for food lovers**, with some of the island's best seafood tavernas.
- **Close to Kimolos**, with easy ferry access for a day trip to another island.

Recommended Stays in Pollonia:

- **Budget: Tania Milos** – Simple, clean rooms right by the water.
- **Mid-range: Kapetan Tasos Suites** – Elegant suites with Cycladic charm.
- **Luxury: White Pebble Suites** – A stylish boutique hotel with modern design.

4. Beyond the Main Towns – Secluded & Unique Stays

If you prefer **privacy and a deeper connection with nature**, consider staying outside the main towns in **beachfront villas, rural retreats, or traditional fisherman's houses**.

- **Firopotamos** – Tiny but magical, with houses right on the water.
- **Mandrakia** – A postcard-perfect fishing village with colorful boat garages.
- **Lagomandra Beach** – A hidden paradise for ultimate relaxation.

Budget-Friendly Stays: Hostels & Affordable Hotels

Milos isn't as expensive as Mykonos or Santorini, but finding **affordable places to stay can still be tricky in peak season**. If you're traveling on a budget, here's where you'll find **comfortable, well-priced accommodations**:

- **Glarakia Studios (Adamas)** – Clean, charming rooms with a garden.

- **Milos Hotel (Adamas)** – A budget-friendly stay with easy ferry access.
- **Hibiscus Rooms (Plaka)** – A cozy, family-run guesthouse in the heart of Plaka.

Tip: Book **at least 3-4 months in advance** if you're visiting in **July or August**, as the best budget stays filled up quickly!

Boutique & Luxury Accommodations

Milos has some **extraordinary accommodations**, from **boutique cave hotels carved into the cliffs** to **private villas overlooking the Aegean Sea**.

- **Milos Cove** – A 5-star luxury resort with infinity pools and spa treatments.
- **Artemis Deluxe Rooms** – Stylish beachfront suites with private pools.
- **Salt Suites & Executive Rooms** – Ultra-modern cave-style suites in Pollonia.

If you're **celebrating a honeymoon, anniversary, or just want to indulge**, these stays are **worth every penny**.

Family-Friendly Stays in Milos

Milos is **one of the most family-friendly Greek islands**, with **calm beaches, safe swimming spots, and plenty of space for kids to explore**. If you're traveling with children, here are the best places to stay:

- **Delmar Apartments & Suites (Pollonia)** – Spacious, family-friendly apartments near the beach.
- **Santa Maria Village (Adamas)** – A great hotel with a big pool and gardens.
- **Glaronisia Hotel (Pollonia)** – Quiet, comfortable, and close to kid-friendly beaches.

Tip: Pollonia is the best area for families, as the **beaches are shallow and safe** for children.

Unique Stays: Traditional Fishermen's Houses & Secluded Villas

Want to stay **somewhere truly special**? Milos has **one-of-a-kind accommodations** that offer an **authentic island experience**.

1. Fishermen's Houses (Syrmata) – Sleep Right on the Water

Milos is famous for **its colorful "syrmata"—tiny boat garages turned into cozy seaside homes**. Staying in one means waking up **just steps from the Aegean**, in a setting that feels straight out of a dream.

- **Best Areas:** Firopotamos, Mandrakia, Klima.
- **Recommended Stay: Blue Mare Apartments (Klima)** – A beautiful house right on the water.

2. Remote & Private Villas – Ultimate Seclusion

If you crave **privacy and uninterrupted sea views**, renting a **secluded villa** is the way to go.

- **White Coast Pool Suites** – A stunning villa with a private infinity pool.
- **Villa Windmill (Tripiti)** – A unique stay in a converted windmill.

Final Thoughts: Choosing the Perfect Stay in Milos

Where you stay in Milos **sets the tone for your adventure**. Whether you prefer **the lively energy of Adamas, the romance of Plaka, the seaside charm of Pollonia, or a remote escape**, there's **a perfect stay for you**.

If you want **convenience and accessibility, Adamas is best**.

 If you're looking for **romance and charm, Plaka is the way to go**.

 If you dream of **peaceful beachfront mornings, Pollonia is your haven**.

 And if you want **something truly unique, a fisherman's house or a secluded villa** will make your trip unforgettable.

No matter where you choose to stay, Milos has a way of **making you feel at home**. And that's what makes this island so special.

Top Must-See Attractions in Milos

Milos isn't just another Greek island—it's an island **that tells a story**. Every cliff, cave, and shoreline holds secrets from the past, whispering tales of pirates, ancient civilizations, and dramatic natural forces that shaped its surreal landscape. I remember the first time I set foot on Milos; I was struck by its **raw beauty** and the sheer variety of landscapes. This isn't an island of just sandy beaches and blue-domed churches. **It's wilder. It's more mysterious. And it's waiting to be explored.**

If you're visiting Milos, these **five must-see attractions** will not only **impress you visually** but **immerse you in history, adventure, and natural wonder**. And trust me—you won't just be checking places off a list. You'll be making memories that will stay with you long after you've left.

Sarakiniko Beach: The Lunar Landscape

I had seen pictures of **Sarakiniko Beach** before visiting, but nothing prepared me for the

otherworldly beauty of actually being there. As I stepped onto the smooth, white volcanic rock, I felt like I had **landed on the moon**. The landscape was **surreal**, with **waves crashing against stark white cliffs, sculpted by time and wind**.

The Story Behind Sarakiniko

Sarakiniko gets its name from the **Saracen pirates** who once used this eerie coastline as a hideout. Standing there, looking at the deep sea caves carved into the cliffs, I imagined the **ghostly figures of pirates** watching the horizon, waiting for the next ship to plunder. Today, the only thing lurking in those caves is the occasional daring swimmer, exploring the labyrinthine tunnels beneath the surface.

What Makes It Special?

- **The stark white rock formations** contrast beautifully with the deep blue sea, making it one of the most photographed spots in Greece.
- **The natural rock pools** are perfect for swimming, with water so clear you can see every pebble beneath.
- **Cliff jumping** is popular here, and if you're feeling adventurous, you can join

the locals in leaping from the lower ledges into the sea.

Best time to visit? Early morning or late afternoon when the sun is lower, casting dramatic shadows across the rocks. And don't forget your camera—this is a place that begs to be captured.

Kleftiko: The Pirate's Hideout

If Sarakiniko is Milos' **moonlike wonder**, then **Kleftiko is its secret hideaway**, a place where history and adventure collide. Getting there isn't easy—you'll need to **take a boat** or embark on a **challenging hike**—but when you finally see those towering white rock formations rising from the turquoise waters, you'll know **it was worth every effort**.

A Place of Pirates and Legends

"Kleftiko" comes from the Greek word **"kleftes"**, meaning thieves. And for centuries, this dramatic cove was a **safe haven for pirates** who used its sea caves to stash their loot. I like to imagine them sitting in their hidden chambers, counting stolen gold while the echoes of the sea filled the caves around them.

What Makes It Special?

- **It's accessible only by boat**, which makes arriving feel like discovering a secret treasure.
- **The caves and tunnels** are incredible for snorkeling and diving—you'll find hidden chambers with sunlight streaming through, illuminating the seabed in a dazzling display of blues and greens.
- **The water is impossibly clear**, with shades of turquoise that don't even seem real.

Tip: Take a **sunset boat tour**—as the light fades, Kleftiko turns into something magical, with the golden hues of the sun reflecting off the white cliffs.

Ancient Theater of Milos

Milos isn't just about **stunning beaches**; it's also home to **rich historical treasures**. One of the most remarkable is the **Ancient Theater of Milos**, a place where you can sit in the very same seats as ancient Greeks did **over 2,000 years ago**.

A Stage for the Gods

Built during the **Hellenistic period**, the theater was later expanded by the **Romans**, turning it into a **grand amphitheater** with stunning views over the Aegean Sea. It's said that **thousands once gathered here** to watch performances, political speeches, and even gladiatorial battles. I remember standing at the very center of the stage, closing my eyes, and imagining the roar of the ancient crowd.

What Makes It Special?

- **The marble seats** have been beautifully preserved, and you can still see the original structure.
- **The panoramic view of the sea** makes it one of the most breathtaking ancient sites in Greece.
- **It's close to the spot where the Venus de Milo was discovered**, one of the most famous sculptures in history, now displayed in the Louvre.

Pro Tip: Visit early in the morning for **an intimate experience**—you'll often have the entire theater to yourself.

Catacombs of Milos: Early Christian History

When I first entered the **Catacombs of Milos**, I felt a deep sense of reverence. The air was cool, the light was dim, and the silence was **almost sacred**. These underground tunnels, dating back to the **1st century AD**, served as **one of the earliest Christian burial sites** in Greece. They are **older than Rome's famous catacombs**, making them a **remarkable piece of history**.

A Hidden World Beneath the Earth

Walking through the labyrinth of tunnels, I could see the carved-out **niches in the walls** where early Christians **secretly worshipped and buried their dead** during times of persecution. The flickering candlelight of my guide cast eerie shadows, making the experience even more haunting.

What Makes It Special?

- **It's one of the most significant early Christian sites in the world.**
- **Over 2,000 people were buried here**, making it a place rich in history and mystery.

- **The underground tunnels feel like stepping back in time**—a must for history lovers.

Best time to visit? Late afternoon, when the shadows add to the mystical ambiance.

Venetian Castle of Plaka: Stunning Sunset Views

If there's **one place in Milos** that will make you **fall in love with the island**, it's the **Venetian Castle of Plaka**. Perched on the highest point of the island, this castle is **more than just a historic ruin**—it's a place to witness **one of the best sunsets in Greece**.

A Fortress with a View

The Venetians built this castle in the **13th century** as a defense against pirates and invaders. Today, only parts of the structure remain, but the view from the top is **nothing short of legendary**. As I climbed the winding stone paths to the peak, I passed **quaint whitewashed chapels** and **vibrant bougainvillea-covered homes** before finally reaching the summit. And when I did, I stood in awe.

The Sunset of a Lifetime

Imagine this: The sky begins to glow with **deep oranges, purples, and reds**. The Aegean Sea stretches endlessly before you, and the entire island is bathed in a warm, golden light. The **wind carries the distant sounds of church bells** from the village below.

It's the kind of view that **stays with you forever**.

What Makes It Special?

- **The best panoramic view on the island**, perfect for photography.
- **A historical site that brings you closer to Milos' medieval past.**
- **An incredible sunset that rivals even Santorini's famous views.**

Pro Tip: Arrive **an hour before sunset** to grab a good spot—this place gets crowded!

Final Thoughts: Exploring Milos' Wonders

Milos is an island of contrasts. **It's raw and untouched, yet rich in history. It's wild and dramatic, yet peaceful and inviting.** Every attraction here **tells a story**, whether it's the **pirate legends of Kleftiko, the ancient performances in the theater, or the spiritual echoes of the catacombs**.

Visiting these places isn't just about sightseeing—it's about **experiencing the magic of Milos firsthand**.

And once you do, I promise you: **You'll never see Greece the same way again.**

Hidden Gems & Off-the-Beaten-Path Spots in Milos

There's something exhilarating about **unearthing a secret**, something known only to those willing to seek it out. While Milos dazzles visitors with its **iconic landmarks and famous beaches,** its true soul lies in the **hidden places**—the ones whispered about among locals, found only by those **who venture off the well-trodden path.**

I remember my first trip to Milos. I had already fallen for its **dramatic cliffs, sapphire waters, and surreal landscapes**, but it wasn't until I started **exploring its hidden corners** that I truly understood the island's magic. Some places felt like stepping into **another world**, while others held the **faint echoes of the past**—abandoned villages, mysterious caves, and silent shores where time seems to stand still.

This is the **Milos that few get to see**. Let's step into the unknown together.

Sykia Cave: A Hidden Natural Wonder

There are caves... and then there is **Sykia Cave**. This isn't just any sea cave—it's **an unearthly sanctuary**, a place where nature has crafted something truly spectacular. And the best part? **There's no roof.**

The Journey to Sykia

Getting to Sykia is **an adventure in itself**. The cave is only accessible **by boat**, and as you approach, you'll notice **a jagged opening in the limestone cliffs**—almost like the mouth of a sleeping giant. The sea narrows into a small entrance, and as your boat carefully navigates through, **the cave suddenly opens up into a breathtaking amphitheater of light and shadow**.

Inside the Cave: A World Apart

I remember stepping into the shallow water, the sun pouring through the collapsed roof, illuminating the **emerald and turquoise hues of the water**. The cave walls, worn smooth by time and tide, **glisten with mystery**. It's easy to imagine that this place was once a **sacred retreat for ancient**

seafarers, a hidden world away from prying eyes.

Why It's Special

- **The natural skylight** creates a magical interplay of light and water.
- **Crystal-clear waters** make it perfect for swimming and snorkeling.
- **It's rarely crowded**, making it one of the most serene places in Milos.

Pro Tip: Visit in the morning when the sun is high, casting an ethereal glow over the water. You'll feel like you've stumbled into a place untouched by time.

Tsigrado Beach: A Beach for the Adventurous

Some beaches invite you in gently. **Tsigrado Beach challenges you.** This is **not** a beach for the faint-hearted—it demands a sense of adventure, a willingness to embrace **both thrill and beauty**.

The Descent: A Test of Courage

I remember standing at the **top of the cliff**, staring down at the **golden sand and**

electric-blue waters below. The only way down? **A series of ladders and ropes, attached precariously to the rocks.** My heart raced as I gripped the wooden rungs, feeling the weight of my decision. But the moment my feet **touched the warm sand**, I knew it was worth it.

The Untouched Beauty of Tsigrado

Tsigrado is **a hidden cove**, sheltered by towering cliffs that make it feel **utterly secluded**. The water here is **so clear that you can see the patterns of the sand below**. There are no sunbeds, no beach bars—just **you, the sea, and the sound of the waves against the cliffs**.

Why It's Special

- **The dramatic descent** makes reaching the beach an achievement.
- **The water is incredibly clear**, perfect for snorkeling.
- **It remains largely untouched**, a secret haven for those willing to find it.

Pro Tip: Wear sturdy shoes for the climb down, and don't bring too much—**your hands will need to be free!**

Kalogries Beach: A Quiet Escape

There's a moment, as you step onto **Kalogries Beach**, when the world seems to **hold its breath**. Maybe it's the way the **cliffs cradle the bay**, or the way the **water shimmers in impossible shades of blue**, but this beach feels **like a dream suspended in time**.

Reaching Kalogries

Unlike the dramatic descent of Tsigrado, Kalogries is **only accessible by boat or a rugged dirt path**. If you're lucky enough to arrive by water, you'll first spot the **gentle, pale sands framed by the untouched cliffs**—a sight that immediately soothes the soul.

Why It's Special

- **The shallow waters are unbelievably clear**, creating the perfect natural swimming pool.
- **It's blissfully quiet**, away from the crowds.
- **The surrounding cliffs shield it from the wind**, making it one of the calmest spots on the island.

Pro Tip: Bring your own food and drinks—there are no facilities here, just **pure, unspoiled beauty.**

The Ghost Village of Zefyria

Milos isn't just about beaches—it holds **secrets from the past**, too. And one of its most intriguing is the **abandoned village of Zefyria**.

The Forgotten Capital

Once upon a time, Zefyria was the **capital of Milos**, a thriving town filled with **churches, markets, and life**. But then, **disaster struck**. In the 18th century, **a massive earthquake** and subsequent plague forced residents to flee, leaving behind **a ghost town, slowly swallowed by time**.

Walking Through a Haunting Past

Today, wandering through Zefyria is like stepping into **an old, forgotten world**. The **ruins of homes and churches stand eerily silent**, with nature reclaiming what was once man's domain. The only structure still in use is the **Church of Panagia Portiani**, a relic of the town's former glory.

Why It's Special

- **It's a glimpse into Milos' past**, frozen in time.
- **It's largely unknown to tourists**, offering a truly eerie and peaceful exploration.
- **The silence here is profound**, broken only by the wind through the ruins.

Pro Tip: Visit at sunset, when the fading light makes the ruins **even more mysterious**.

Remote Fishing Villages: Skinopi, Mandrakia & Firopotamos

While most visitors flock to the **bustling villages of Adamas and Pollonia**, the real magic of Milos lies in its **tiny fishing settlements**, where **time slows down and the sea is king**.

Skinopi: A Village on the Water

Skinopi is **barely a village at all**, more like a **collection of boat houses clinging to the shoreline**. The houses, known as **"syrmata"**, are painted in **bright blues, reds, and yellows**, their doors opening directly onto the sea. Fishermen still **store their boats inside these cave-like homes**, just as they have for centuries.

Mandrakia: The Quintessential Fishing Haven

Mandrakia is **postcard-perfect**. The tiny harbor, with its **turquoise waters and colorful syrmata**, is **one of the most peaceful spots on the island**. I remember sitting at a seaside taverna, watching the fishermen mend their nets, the scent of **grilled octopus and salt in the air**.

Firopotamos: A Secluded Gem

Tucked away between rocky cliffs, **Firopotamos is the kind of place that steals your heart**. A handful of **fishermen's homes sit along the shore**, their reflections dancing in the calm bay. There's **a small, whitewashed chapel**, a reminder of the village's deep-rooted traditions.

Why These Villages Are Special

- **They offer a glimpse into the authentic fishing life of Milos.**

- They are quiet, unspoiled, and unbelievably picturesque.
- Each has a charm of its own, from Skinopi's sea caves to Mandrakia's postcard-perfect harbor.

Pro Tip: Visit early in the morning for **a magical sunrise experience**.

Final Thoughts: Milos' Hidden Soul

Milos is an island that **rewards the curious**, the ones willing to **go beyond the obvious**. From **secret caves to abandoned villages, from secluded beaches to timeless fishing hamlets**, these hidden gems are **where the island's true magic lies**.

And now that you know about them, **it's time to start your own journey into the unknown.**

Exploring Milos by Sea

There's something about being out in the **open water**, the salty breeze in your hair, and the endless blue stretching all around you that makes you feel **truly alive**. And in Milos—an island sculpted by **volcanic forces, winds, and waves**—the best way to experience its raw beauty is from the **sea itself**.

Some places **can't be reached by road**, and some secrets are hidden **beneath the surface**, waiting for those **bold enough to dive in**. From **thrilling boat tours** to **sunset sails**, from **kayaking past sea caves** to **diving into crystal-clear waters**, exploring Milos by sea is an **adventure you'll never forget**.

Let's set sail, shall we?

Best Boat Tours: Full-Day & Half-Day Cruises

If you want to **see Milos at its most breathtaking**, you need to **get on a boat**. Whether it's a **half-day tour to hidden beaches** or a **full-day cruise around the**

island, a boat trip is **the ultimate way** to experience the dramatic coastlines, sea caves, and legendary pirate hideouts.

Full-Day Boat Tours: The Ultimate Exploration

A **full-day cruise** is **the best way** to circle the entire island and uncover spots that are **completely inaccessible by land**. These tours typically start from **Adamas or Pollonia**, sailing past **the lunar cliffs of Sarakiniko, the remote shores of Agios Ioannis, and the mysterious waters of Sykia Cave.**

But the highlight of any full-day cruise?
Kleftiko.

This **legendary cove**, once a hideout for pirates, is a maze of **white limestone formations, natural arches, and secret caves**. The water here is **so crystal-clear that you can see straight to the bottom**. Most tours stop here for a long swim break, and some even offer **snorkeling equipment** so you can **explore the underwater tunnels and caves**.

Half-Day Boat Tours: Quick but Spectacular

If you're short on time, a **half-day cruise** will still take you to some of **Milos' most beautiful spots**. Many half-day tours focus on either the **south coast (including Kleftiko and Sykia Cave)** or the **north side (featuring Sarakiniko and Polyaigos Island)**.

These shorter tours are **ideal for those who want a taste of adventure** but still **leave time for other island activities**.

Why a Boat Tour is a Must-Do in Milos

- You'll visit places **only accessible by sea**.
- **Swimming in Kleftiko** is an unforgettable experience.
- Many tours include **traditional Greek food and drinks**, making it a **full sensory experience**.

Pro Tip: Book in advance, especially in **peak summer months**, as these tours fill up fast!

Snorkeling & Scuba Diving Hotspots

There's a whole other world **beneath the waves**, and Milos has some of the **most fascinating underwater landscapes in Greece**. The volcanic seabed has created a **stunning marine ecosystem**, with **hidden caves, colorful coral formations, and sunken wrecks** waiting to be explored.

Best Snorkeling Spots in Milos

- **Kleftiko:** The underwater **tunnels and arches** make this an incredible spot to snorkel. The **visibility is stunning**, and you'll often see **shoals of tiny fish darting between the rocks**.
- **Tsigrado Beach:** The **calm, shallow waters** make this perfect for spotting **small fish and interesting rock formations**.
- **Gerakas Beach:** This **remote beach**, accessible only by boat, has some of the **clearest waters you'll ever see**. Snorkeling here feels like floating in **a giant aquarium**.

Scuba Diving Adventures

For those looking to go **deeper**, scuba diving in Milos offers **incredible volcanic rock formations, caves, and even shipwrecks**. One of the best diving spots is **the wreck of a German World War II airplane**, resting on the seabed **just off the coast**.

Other dive sites include:

- **Papafragas Caves:** A series of **dramatic underwater tunnels**.
- **Agios Dimitrios Reef:** A great place to see **sea turtles, octopuses, and vibrant marine life**.
- **Kalogries Bay:** Perfect for **beginner divers**, with **calm waters and plenty of marine biodiversity**.

Pro Tip: Milos has **several great dive centers** offering **guided dives and certification courses**—perfect for beginners and experienced divers alike!

Kayaking Along the Coastline

If you prefer to **explore at your own pace**, nothing beats **kayaking along the coast of Milos**. The island's coastline is a **playground of caves, arches, and hidden coves**, and a kayak lets you **slip into places boats can't reach**.

Best Kayaking Routes in Milos

- **Sarakiniko to Papafragas:** This **north coast route** takes you past **moon-like rock formations, sea caves, and dramatic cliffs**.
- **Kleftiko by Kayak:** Paddling into **Kleftiko's caves** is a completely different experience from arriving by boat. You can explore **every little nook and cranny**, finding spots where even the tour boats can't go!
- **Pollonia to Kimolos:** For the ultimate adventure, kayak across to the **neighboring island of Kimolos**, stopping at **hidden beaches along the way**.

Kayaking is **both peaceful and exhilarating**—it's just you, the sea, and the quiet rhythm of your paddle slicing through the water.

Pro Tip: Go early in the morning when the **waters are calmer**, and always check the **wind conditions** before heading out!

Sunset Sailing & Luxury Yacht Experiences

Milos is **one of the best places in Greece to experience a sunset at sea**. The sky turns **gold, pink, and deep purple**, and the water reflects it all like **liquid fire**. If you want a **romantic and unforgettable experience**, a **sunset sailing trip** is **a must**.

Why Choose a Sunset Sail?

- The sea is **calm and peaceful in the evening**.
- The **changing colors of the cliffs and water** at sunset are **breathtaking**.
- Some tours offer **champagne and gourmet snacks**, making it **a luxurious experience**.

For those who prefer **a more exclusive adventure**, private yacht charters are available for **tailor-made experiences**, including **personalized routes, gourmet dining, and even overnight stays on board**.

Island Hopping from Milos

Milos isn't the only gem in the Cyclades. From here, you can hop over to **neighboring islands**, each offering something unique.

Top Island Hopping Destinations

- **Kimolos:** A **quiet, authentic island** with **traditional whitewashed houses and uncrowded beaches**.
- **Polyaigos:** An **uninhabited paradise** with some of the **clearest waters in the Aegean**.
- **Sifnos:** Known for its **gourmet food scene and charming villages**.

Pro Tip: Many boat tours **combine Milos, Polyaigos, and Kimolos** into a **single-day excursion**, giving you a taste of multiple islands in one trip.

Final Thoughts: The Call of the Sea

Exploring Milos by sea isn't just an activity—it's **an adventure that awakens the soul**. Whether you're **sailing past towering cliffs**, **snorkeling through hidden caves**, or **kayaking into secret coves**, the experience of being on the water here is **beyond magical**.

The **Aegean is calling**, and Milos is waiting.
Are you ready to answer?

Best Beaches in Milos

There's something about the beaches of Milos that **feels otherworldly**. It's not just the **soft sands or the crystal-clear waters**, though they are **some of the best in Greece**. It's the way the **landscapes shift** from one beach to the next—**dramatic white cliffs, fiery red rocks, golden sands, and secret coves** that feel like they were sculpted **just for you**.

Lying on a beach in Milos isn't just about **basking in the sun**. It's about **experiencing** the island's **volcanic soul**, feeling the history in the stones, and letting the **gentle waves lull you into a dreamlike state**.

Let's take a journey to the most **breathtaking beaches of Milos**—places where time slows down, and the sea whispers stories of **ancient myths and sun-drenched afternoons**.

Sarakiniko Beach: The Famous White Volcanic Cliffs

I'll never forget the first time I set foot on **Sarakiniko Beach**. It was like stepping onto the **surface of the moon**. The **smooth, white volcanic rock stretched out in every direction**, sculpted by the wind and waves into **bizarre, otherworldly formations**.

The contrast is **breathtaking**—the stark **white cliffs against the deep, endless blue of the Aegean Sea**. The water here is

unbelievably clear, a shimmering turquoise that invites you to dive in.

The Experience

- Walking along the **chalky cliffs** feels surreal, like you're exploring **a dreamlike landscape**.
- Jumping into the **cool, transparent waters** from one of the **low rock ledges** is an exhilarating thrill.
- At sunset, the **white rocks turn soft shades of pink and orange**, casting an **almost magical glow**.

This is not just a **beach for sunbathing**—it's a place to **wander, explore, and get lost in the beauty of nature's artistry**.

Firiplaka Beach: Colorful Cliffs & Crystal Waters

If there's a place that **embodies pure relaxation**, it's **Firiplaka Beach**. Unlike the moon-like white of Sarakiniko, Firiplaka is a **kaleidoscope of colors**. The **cliffs rise high behind you, streaked with shades of red, orange, pink, and yellow**—a volcanic masterpiece.

Then there's the **water**. Oh, the water! It's that perfect shade of **electric blue**, so clear you can see **the sandy bottom even when you're floating far from shore**.

The Experience

- The **golden sand** is warm and soft underfoot, **perfect for lounging**.
- The **shallow waters** are ideal for a **leisurely swim**.
- The **beach bar** offers ice-cold drinks—**a must on a hot summer day**.

Firiplaka has an **effortless, laid-back vibe**, perfect for spending **an entire afternoon soaking in the beauty**.

Papafragas Beach: A Natural Swimming Pool

Some beaches feel **secret**, like they were meant to be **discovered rather than simply visited. Papafragas Beach is one of those places**.

Nestled between **towering volcanic walls**, this beach is more of a **natural swimming pool than a traditional shoreline. A narrow channel of crystal-clear water** leads out to the open sea, framed by **rocky cliffs and hidden caves**.

The Experience

- Walking down the **rocky path** to reach the beach feels like **stepping into a hidden paradise**.
- Floating in the **calm, deep turquoise waters** between the cliffs is **an almost meditative experience**.
- Exploring the **sea caves** nearby adds a sense of **adventure and mystery**.

This is the kind of place that makes you **pause, breathe deeply, and truly appreciate the magic of nature**.

Paleochori Beach: Hot Springs & Multi Colored Rocks

Paleochori Beach isn't just a **place to sunbathe**—it's a place where you can **literally feel the earth's power beneath you**. Thanks to **geothermal activity**, the sands here are **naturally heated,** and if you step into the shallow waters, you might feel **warm currents rising from underwater hot springs**.

And then there are the **cliffs**. They **glow in shades of red, gold, and violet**, a reminder of the **island's volcanic origins**.

The Experience

- The **geothermal waters** create **a natural spa-like experience**.
- The **small beachfront tavernas** serve **seafood grilled over volcanic stones**, giving it a **unique smoky flavor**.
- The **long, spacious shoreline** makes it **perfect for those who love quiet beach walks**.

Paleochori is where you go to **immerse yourself in the natural elements**, feeling the **heat of the earth and the coolness of the sea in one magical moment**.

Agia Kyriaki Beach: Family-Friendly Relaxation

Not all of Milos' beaches are about **dramatic landscapes and hidden coves**. Some are simply **perfect for a long, lazy day under the sun**, and **Agia Kyriaki Beach** is one of the best.

This beach has **soft, golden sand, gentle waves**, and plenty of **space to spread out**. It's an ideal place for **families, couples, or solo travelers looking for a stress-free beach day**.

The Experience

- The **calm waters** are perfect for **floating and unwinding**.
- There are **sunbeds and umbrellas**, making it **easy to spend the whole day here**.
- The **tavernas nearby** serve some of the **best fresh seafood on the island**.

Sometimes, the best beach experiences are the **simple ones**—soft sand, **warm sun**, and the **gentle sound of the waves** lapping at the shore.

Final Thoughts: A Beach for Every Mood

One of the most beautiful things about Milos is that **every beach offers something different**.

- When I want to feel like I'm on **another planet**, I go to **Sarakiniko**.
- When I crave **colorful cliffs and relaxed swimming**, I head to **Firiplaka**.
- When I seek **hidden beauty**, **Papafragas** calls my name.
- When I want to experience **Milos' volcanic soul**, I find it at **Paleochori**.

- And when I just need a **stress-free beach day**, **Agia Kyriaki** is my go-to.

Milos isn't just a place you **visit**—it's a place you **feel**. And there's no better way to experience it than by **sinking your toes into its warm sands and letting the Aegean Sea carry your worries away**.

Are you ready to find your **perfect beach in Milos?**

Food & Drink: Where & What to Eat in Milos

There's something about the food in Milos that makes every meal feel like a **celebration**. Maybe it's the **freshness of the ingredients**, the **rich traditions** passed down through generations, or the simple joy of **eating by the sea**, with a salty breeze brushing against your skin.

Every bite here tells a **story**—of sun-drenched farms, hardworking fishermen, and the **deep culinary heritage** of the Cyclades. Whether it's a **crisp, golden cheese pie**, a plate of **grilled octopus**, or a spoonful of **sweet watermelon pie**, the flavors of Milos are **pure magic**.

Join me on a **mouthwatering journey** through the best dishes, tavernas, and places to sip a drink as the sun sets over the Aegean.

Traditional Milos Dishes You Must Try

Greek food is **legendary**, but Milos has its own **distinct flavors** that set it apart from the rest of the Cyclades. Here are some **must-try local specialties** that capture the island's **essence**.

Pitarakia (Milos Cheese Pies)

I still remember my **first bite of pitarakia**—the warm, flaky pastry **crumbled in my mouth**, releasing the rich, slightly tangy flavor of **local Milos cheese**. These small, golden pies are made with **hand-rolled dough** and filled with **mizithra cheese**, a soft, slightly salty cheese that melts beautifully when baked.

The secret? Many families **add their own twist**—a touch of mint, a hint of honey, or a sprinkle of sesame seeds. Every taverna makes them **slightly differently**, so you'll want to **try them more than once!**

Karpouzopita (Watermelon Pie)

Yes, you read that right—**watermelon pie**. It's a uniquely **Milos dessert**, made from **juicy local watermelon**, honey, cinnamon, and flour, baked until it's caramelized and **almost jam-like**. The **sweetness is natural,** the texture is soft and slightly chewy, and it pairs perfectly with **a scoop of fresh Greek yogurt**.

This is a dessert that tastes like **summer in Greece**. One bite, and you'll be **hooked**.

Ladenia

If Greece had its own version of **pizza**, this would be it. Ladenia is a **rustic, oven-baked flatbread** topped with **fresh tomatoes,**

onions, and olive oil. The ingredients are so simple, yet the flavors are **incredible**. The tomatoes **roast to perfection**, the onions **turn sweet**, and the olive oil soaks into the bread, making every bite **unforgettable**.

It's the **perfect snack** for a day at the beach or a quick bite before dinner.

Gouna (Sun-Dried Mackerel)

This is **Milos' ultimate seafood delicacy**. Fresh mackerel is **butterflied, salted, and left to dry under the Greek sun**, then grilled until it's **crispy on the outside, tender and smoky on the inside**. It pairs beautifully with a **chilled glass of ouzo or white wine**.

It's a dish that **tastes like the Aegean itself**—salty, fresh, and full of character.

Best Tavernas for Authentic Greek Cuisine

The best meals in Milos aren't found in **fancy restaurants**. They're in **family-run tavernas**, where grandmothers still **stir the pots**, and recipes haven't changed for

generations. Here are some of my **favorite spots for an unforgettable meal**.

Medusa (Mandrakia)

Perched on the **edge of the sea**, Medusa serves up some of the **freshest seafood on the island**. Their **grilled octopus** is legendary—tender, smoky, and served with a drizzle of **lemon and olive oil**. Pair it with a glass of **ouzo**, and you've got a meal that's **pure Greek bliss**.

Glaronisia (Tripiti)

A warm, welcoming taverna known for its **homemade Greek dishes**. Their **moussaka** is a must-try—layers of **eggplant, minced meat, and creamy béchamel**, baked to **golden perfection**. It's **comfort food at its finest**.

O Hamos (Adamas)

If you want **authentic Milos cuisine**, this is the place to go. Everything here is **homemade**, from the **freshly baked bread** to the **slow-cooked lamb in tomato sauce**. The menu is **handwritten**, the portions are **huge**, and the flavors are **unforgettable**.

Seafood Specialties & Waterfront Dining

Milos is an **island of fishermen**, which means the seafood here is **some of the best in Greece**. You'll find it grilled, baked, stewed, or served **straight from the sea to your plate**.

Grilled Octopus

There's something almost **ceremonial** about eating **grilled octopus in Greece**. The **tentacles, charred and crisp on the outside, are unbelievably tender inside**. A squeeze of **fresh lemon**, a drizzle of **olive oil**, and a sprinkle of oregano—it's simple, **but the flavors explode in your mouth**.

Stuffed Squid

Fresh squid is **grilled whole**, stuffed with a **mixture of feta cheese, tomatoes, and herbs**. The squid is **tender and smoky**, the filling **melts in your mouth**, and it all comes together **beautifully**.

Sea Urchin Salad

A true **local delicacy**, sea urchins are cracked open, revealing their **golden roe**—a taste of the **purest, freshest seafood imaginable**. It's served with **olive oil, lemon, and crusty bread**.

Must-Try Local Sweets & Desserts

Melopita (Honey Pie)

A sweet, creamy **cheesecake-like dessert**, made with **local mizithra cheese and honey**. It's light, fragrant, and **absolutely delicious**.

Pasteli (Sesame & Honey Bars)

A traditional Greek snack made from **honey and sesame seeds**, pressed into **crisp golden bars**. It's the perfect **sweet treat** after a meal.

Best Bars & Cafés for Drinks with a View

Utopia Café (Plaka)

There's no better place to **watch the sunset** than from the terrace of **Utopia Café**. Perched high in Plaka, it offers **breathtaking views** over the **Aegean**, best enjoyed with a **glass of crisp white wine or a strong Greek coffee**.

Akri Bar (Adamas)

If you're in the mood for a **cocktail by the sea**, Akri Bar is the place to go. Their **signature mojitos**, made with **fresh Greek herbs**, are **refreshing and delicious**.

Enalion (Pollonia)

A **charming waterfront café** where you can sip a **Greek frappé or a glass of ouzo**, watching the **fishing boats bob on the water**.

Final Thoughts: A Culinary Journey You Won't Forget

Milos isn't just an island of **beautiful beaches and hidden caves**—it's an island of **flavors, traditions, and unforgettable meals**. From **cheese pies and grilled octopus** to **watermelon pie and honey-drizzled desserts**, every bite here tells a **story of history, culture, and love for food**.

So when you come to Milos, **come hungry**. Because **every meal is an experience**, and every bite is a **taste of paradise**.

Culture & History of Milos

Walking through Milos is like stepping into a **living history book**. Every path, every ruin, every artifact tells a **story of civilizations that thrived here**—from the **ancient Greeks and Romans to early Christians and Venetian rulers**.

But culture isn't just found in **museums or ancient sites**—it's alive in the **traditions, festivals, and everyday life of the islanders**. I've always believed that to truly know a place, you have to **listen to its past and immerse yourself in its present**. So let's take a journey through the **culture and history of Milos**, from its archaeological treasures to its **vibrant local traditions**.

Archaeological Museum of Milos

The **Archaeological Museum of Milos**, housed in a beautiful **neoclassical building** in Plaka, is a treasure trove of **ancient wonders**. Stepping inside, I was greeted by a **stone guardian of history**—a replica of the **Venus de Milo**, the island's most famous masterpiece.

The Marble Marvels of Milos

Milos was famous for its **high-quality marble**, and the sculptures here prove why. Walking through the halls, I saw **statues of gods, warriors, and noblemen**, their expressions frozen in time. Each sculpture revealed the **skill of the island's ancient artisans**, who carved life into cold stone.

Prehistoric Echoes from Phylakopi

One of the museum's highlights is the **collection from Phylakopi**, an ancient city that flourished during the **Bronze Age**. Looking at the **painted pottery and tools**, I imagined the people who once lived here—traders, fishermen, and craftsmen who helped shape **Aegean civilization**.

This museum isn't just a place to see artifacts; it's a place to **understand the soul of Milos through its artistic and historical legacy**.

Folklore Museum of Plaka: A Glimpse into Traditional Milos

Culture isn't just about **ancient ruins**—it's also about the **traditions that survive the test of time**. That's why I love the **Folklore Museum of Plaka**.

Walking into the museum feels like **stepping into a 19th-century Milos home**. The scent of **aged wood and textiles** fills the air, and the rooms are decorated with **handmade furniture, traditional costumes, and old kitchen tools**.

Life in Old Milos

I was fascinated by the **daily objects of island life**—loom-woven fabrics, ceramic plates, and **olive oil lamps** that once lit up the nights. There were **old musical instruments**, too, and I could almost hear the **melodies of traditional Greek songs** that would have filled these homes during celebrations.

The Art of Weaving and Pottery

One of the most interesting sections showcased the island's **pottery and weaving traditions**. Women would spend hours weaving **colorful fabrics**, while potters shaped **jugs and vases from the island's rich' clay**. These crafts, passed down through generations, still influence **Milos' artistic identity today**.

The Venus de Milo: Milos' Most Famous Masterpiece

Even if you've never been to Greece, you've probably seen the **Venus de Milo**—one of the most famous statues in the world. But did you know this breathtaking sculpture was discovered **right here on Milos?**

The Discovery of an Icon

In 1820, a farmer named **Yorgos Kentrotas** was digging on his land when he unearthed something remarkable—**a broken marble statue, buried for centuries**. French sailors, recognizing its **beauty and historical significance**, quickly negotiated its purchase. The statue was soon shipped to France, where it became **one of the Louvre's most prized exhibits**.

What Makes Venus de Milo Special?

This **graceful, armless beauty**, believed to represent **Aphrodite, the goddess of love**, is an icon of **classical Greek art**. Her **mysterious expression**, the **delicate folds of her drapery**, and the **perfect balance of movement and stillness** make her a masterpiece.

But for the people of Milos, the Venus de Milo is more than just **a sculpture in a museum**. She is a **symbol of the island's rich artistic heritage**, and many locals still dream of the day she **returns home**.

Christian Catacombs & Ancient Artifacts

Beneath the **sun-drenched hills of Milos**, an **ancient underground world** tells the story of **early Christianity**. The **Catacombs of Milos**, carved into soft volcanic rock, are some of the **oldest and most significant Christian burial sites in the world**.

A Sacred Place of Worship

Walking into the catacombs, I felt an **immediate hush**, as if the air itself carried the weight of **centuries-old prayers**. The dimly lit tunnels are filled with **rock-cut graves**, where early Christians buried their dead in secret during times of **Roman persecution**.

Some tombs still have **faint carvings of crosses and fish symbols**, early Christian marks of faith. Standing there, I imagined the people who once **gathered here in the dark**, whispering prayers and sharing stories of hope.

Ancient Artifacts of Faith

The site also holds **ancient inscriptions and artifacts**, giving us a glimpse into the **spiritual life of Milos' early Christian community**. These catacombs aren't just burial sites; they are places where **faith and history intertwine**, reminding us of the resilience of those who came before us.

Traditional Festivals & Events in Milos

History may be found in **museums and ruins**, but the heart of a culture beats strongest in its **celebrations**. Milos is home to **vibrant festivals** that bring people together in **joy, music, and tradition**.

The Feast of Agios Charalambos (February 10th)

This is one of the **most important religious celebrations** on the island, dedicated to **Saint Charalambos**, the protector of Milos. Villagers gather for **church services**, followed by **feasts, traditional dancing, and lively music**.

Easter in Milos: A Celebration of Light

Greek Easter is **an unforgettable experience**, and in Milos, it's celebrated with **sacred rituals and joyous traditions**. On **Holy Saturday**, locals gather with **candles in hand**, waiting for the moment when the priest declares **"Christos Anesti!" (Christ is Risen!)**. Fireworks light up the night, and families return home for a **feast of lamb and traditional Easter bread**.

The Festival of Prophet Elias (July 20th)

This festival, held in honor of **Prophet Elias**, takes place in small mountain chapels across Milos. Locals **hike to the chapels**, light candles, and enjoy a **picnic-style feast** with music and dancing.

Panagia Korfiatissa Festival (August 15th)

The **biggest festival of the summer**, dedicated to the **Virgin Mary**, is a time of **prayer, feasting, and celebration**. Families dress in their **best clothes**, attend **church services**, and then gather for a **huge**

island-wide feast. The night ends with **live music, dancing, and fireworks** over the Aegean.

Final Thoughts: Living History & Culture in Milos

Milos is not just an island of **stunning landscapes**—it's an island of **stories, traditions, and enduring spirit**. From the **whispers of ancient civilizations** in the Archaeological Museum to the **warmth of traditional Greek festivals**, every corner of Milos has **a tale to tell**.

Whether you're exploring Venus **de Milo's legacy, descending into the catacombs, or dancing at a village festival**, you're **not just a visitor**—you're a part of the **living history of Milos**.

Adventure & Outdoor Activities in Milos

Milos isn't just a paradise of **white volcanic cliffs and crystal-clear waters**—it's a playground for those of us who crave **adventure, exploration, and the thrill of discovery**. Whether it's hiking across rugged landscapes, **climbing volcanic rock formations, cycling along coastal roads, or even riding a horse by the sea**, this island is made for **those who refuse to sit still**.

I've always believed that the best way to experience a place is to **get outside, push your limits, and embrace the unknown**. So, let's dive into some of the **most exhilarating outdoor activities Milos has to offer!**

Hiking Trails & Best Walking Routes

Milos' **wild, untamed beauty** is best explored on foot. The island is crisscrossed with **ancient trails and scenic paths**, each one leading to **breathtaking viewpoints, hidden beaches, and historical ruins**.

Hiking to Profitis Ilias: The Highest Peak in Milos

If you're up for a challenge, the hike to **Profitis Ilias**—the highest point on the island—is an absolute must. The climb is **moderate to difficult**, but every step is worth it. As I ascended, the air became **crisper, the silence deeper**, and the **360-degree views** at the top were nothing short of **spectacular**. Standing there, looking down at the **Aegean stretching endlessly around me**, I felt like I had conquered the world.

The Ancient Trails of Milos

For history lovers, the island's **ancient paths** offer a blend of **natural beauty and cultural significance**. One of my favorites is the **Plaka to Klima trail**, which winds through **old villages, rolling hills, and ancient ruins** before descending to the **colorful fishing houses of Klima**. As I walked, I imagined the **countless footsteps that had traveled this route before me**—traders, sailors, and villagers from centuries past.

Rock Climbing & Exploring Volcanic Formations

Milos is **volcanic at its core**, and its dramatic rock formations make it a **haven for climbers and thrill-seekers**. Whether you're a **beginner or an experienced climber**, the island offers **incredible opportunities** to test your strength and skill.

Climbing the White Cliffs of Sarakiniko

Sarakiniko is famous for its **lunar-like landscape**, but did you know it's also an **amazing spot for bouldering and free climbing**? The smooth, wind-carved rocks provide **natural grips and ledges**, making it a **dream for climbers**. As I scaled the cliffs, the **salt-scented air and crashing waves below** gave me an **adrenaline rush like no other**.

Exploring the Lava Caves of Milos

For a **different kind of thrill**, I ventured into some of Milos' **lava caves**. These dark, twisting tunnels were formed by ancient volcanic eruptions, and exploring them felt like stepping into **another world**. I squeezed through **narrow rock passages**, my flashlight illuminating the **glowing minerals and strange rock formations** around me.

Every turn was a **new mystery waiting to be uncovered**.

Cycling Around Milos

If you want to **cover more ground** while still immersing yourself in **Milos' stunning landscapes**, cycling is the way to go. The island's **smooth coastal roads and rugged mountain trails** make it **perfect for riders of all skill levels**.

Scenic Coastal Rides

One of my favorite rides takes you from **Adamas to Pollonia**, following the **coastline with breathtaking views of the sea**. The road is mostly **flat and easy**, making it perfect for a **relaxed ride** with plenty of stops for **photos and seaside cafés**.

Mountain Biking in the Wild Interior

For those who crave **more intensity**, the trails through Milos' **rocky interior** offer an **unforgettable off-road experience**. Riding through **dusty paths, past abandoned mines, and across rolling hills**, I felt like a true explorer. The challenge of navigating **steep inclines and rugged terrain** was

exhilarating, and reaching the top of a hill to see the **entire island spread out below me** was the ultimate reward.

Horseback Riding by the Sea

There's something **magical** about experiencing Milos **on horseback**. The island's **gentle terrain and open landscapes** make it perfect for **leisurely rides through nature** or along **secluded beaches at sunset**.

A Sunset Ride Along Agia Kyriaki Beach

One evening, I joined a small **horseback riding tour** along **Agia Kyriaki Beach**. As the sun dipped below the horizon, my horse's hooves splashed through the shallow waves, and a warm breeze carried the **salty scent of the sea**. It was a moment of **pure tranquility**—just me, my horse, and the endless sky.

Exploring the Rolling Hills of Milos

For a more adventurous ride, I ventured into the **olive groves and rocky hills** around **Zefyria**. Trotting through ancient trails, past **ruins and tiny whitewashed chapels**, I felt like I had traveled **back in time**. The connection between **rider and horse**, the sound of hooves on the earth, and the **breathtaking scenery** made it an **unforgettable experience**.

Photography Hotspots for Stunning Views

For those who love **capturing the beauty of nature**, Milos is **a paradise of breathtaking landscapes and golden light**. Whether you're a professional photographer or just someone who loves snapping amazing shots, the island is filled with **picture-perfect locations**.

Sarakiniko's Otherworldly Terrain

Sarakiniko is **the most photographed place in Milos**, and for good reason. Its **smooth, bone-white cliffs against the deep blue sea** look like something **from another planet**. At sunrise or sunset, the light turns the rocks into **shades of pink and gold**, making it a dream for photographers.

Kleftiko: The Hidden Pirate Coves

Accessible only by boat, **Kleftiko's towering white cliffs and sea caves** create a **dramatic backdrop** for any photo. I spent hours here, capturing the way the **light danced on the water**, highlighting the cliffs' **intricate textures and hidden tunnels**.

Plaka's Sunset Panoramas

For the **best sunset view on the island**, nothing beats the **Venetian Castle of Plaka**. Standing at the top of the hill, camera in hand, I watched as the **sky exploded into fiery oranges and purples**, casting a golden glow over the **rooftops and Aegean waters below**. It was the kind of view that makes you feel **alive and inspired**, reminding me why I travel—to witness moments like this.

Final Thoughts: Milos Is an Adventurer's Dream

Milos is not just an island to **visit**—it's an island to **experience**. Whether you're **hiking rugged trails, scaling volcanic cliffs, cycling along the coast, or riding a horse at sunset**, every moment here is an **opportunity for adventure**.

If you crave the **thrill of the outdoors, the rush of exploration, and the beauty of untouched nature**, then **Milos is waiting for you**. So pack your bags, lace up your hiking boots, and get ready to **discover the wild, adventurous spirit of this incredible island**!

Day Trips & Nearby Islands

Milos is a paradise in itself, but if you're anything like me, the urge to **venture beyond the horizon** is irresistible. There's something about setting off from the harbor, watching the island shrink behind you, and feeling that **rush of anticipation** as another island emerges in the distance. The Cyclades are filled with **hidden treasures**, and Milos is the perfect jumping-off point to explore **some of the most enchanting nearby islands**.

Each island has its **own personality**, its own **rhythm**, and its own **magic**. Whether it's the **secluded shores of Polyaigos, the timeless charm of Kimolos, the elegance of Sifnos, or the dramatic cliffs of Folegandros**, these day trips will **transport you to a world of Greek island dreams**.

Kimolos: The Neighboring Hidden Gem

Kimolos is **so close to Milos** that you could almost swim there—but trust me, taking the short **15-minute ferry ride** from Pollonia is a much better idea. The moment I stepped off the boat, I felt like I had **traveled back in time**. Kimolos is one of those islands that **remains untouched by mass tourism**, where life moves at a slower pace, and every turn leads to **another postcard-perfect scene**.

Exploring Chorio: A Village Stuck in Time

The heart of Kimolos is **Chorio**, a **whitewashed maze of narrow alleys, flower-filled courtyards, and charming squares**. As I wandered through, I stumbled upon tiny tavernas serving **home-cooked Greek specialties**, a handful of friendly cats basking in the sun, and locals who greeted me as if they'd known me forever. It's the kind of place where **time seems to stand still**, where you can sit at a café with a Greek coffee and simply watch the world go by.

Prassa Beach: The Caribbean of the Cyclades

I had heard whispers of **Prassa Beach**, a spot so beautiful it's often called the **"Caribbean of the Cyclades."** The rumors were true. The sand was **pure white**, the water **a surreal shade of turquoise**, and the atmosphere

blissfully quiet. I spent the afternoon floating in the crystal-clear sea, feeling like I had discovered a **secret paradise** that only a few lucky travelers ever find.

Polyaigos: Greece's Largest Uninhabited Island

If **seclusion, wild beauty, and untouched nature** call to you, then Polyaigos is your answer. This **uninhabited island**, just a short boat ride from Milos, is a **sanctuary of raw, unspoiled landscapes**. The only residents here? **A handful of goats, sea birds, and the occasional Mediterranean monk seal.**

The Blue Waters of Galazia Nera

I have never seen water **so blue** in my life. The moment the boat pulled into **Galazia Nera**, I was speechless. The sea was so clear that I could see the **rippled sand 10 meters below**. As I dove into the water, it felt like swimming through **liquid sapphire**, an experience so surreal it almost didn't feel real.

Hidden Caves & Dramatic Cliffs

Polyaigos is full of **mystical caves and towering rock formations**, carved by the wind and sea over millennia. One of the most mesmerizing was the **Fanara Cave**, where the sunlight filtered through a small opening, illuminating the water in an eerie, glowing blue. Exploring these caves by **boat, kayak, or even snorkeling** felt like discovering **a lost world**, untouched by time.

Sifnos: A Taste of Cycladic Elegance

Sifnos is **the island of elegance, gastronomy, and charming villages**, and it's just a short ferry ride from Milos. The moment I arrived, I could feel the **difference in atmosphere**—Sifnos has a refined beauty, a kind of **effortless grace** that makes you want to slow down and **savor every moment**.

Apollonia: The Chic Capital

The capital, **Apollonia**, is a place where you could **spend hours just strolling**. Boutique shops line the narrow streets, **selling handmade ceramics, jewelry, and traditional sweets**. I stopped at a café, sipped on a glass of **local wine**, and watched as elegantly dressed locals and visitors **mingled under the soft golden light of the Cycladic sun.**

A Culinary Paradise: The Flavors of Sifnos

Sifnos is known as **the gastronomic capital of the Cyclades**, and I quickly found out why. The island is the birthplace of **Nikolaos Tselementes, Greece's most famous chef**, and his influence lives on in every dish. I devoured a plate of **revithada (slow-cooked chickpea stew)**, followed by a taste of **mastelo (lamb cooked in red wine and herbs)**. Every bite was **a revelation**, a reminder of how **food connects us to a place and its history**.

Folegandros: A Cliffside Escape

Some islands feel **like they belong in a dream**, and Folegandros is one of them. **Dramatic cliffs, a stunning hilltop Chora, and hidden beaches** make this island one of the **most breathtaking in Greece**.

Chora: The Prettiest Village in the Cyclades?

The moment I arrived in **Chora**, I knew I had found **something special**. The village is perched **high above the sea**, with **breathtaking views in every direction**. As I wandered through the **whitewashed streets, past charming squares and bougainvillea-covered houses**, I felt like I had stepped into a **fairy tale**.

The Church of Panagia: A Pilgrimage Worth the Climb

At the very top of the island sits the **Church of Panagia**, accessible by a **steep, winding path**. The climb was tough, but when I reached the top, I was rewarded with a **view that took my breath away**. The sun was setting, casting a golden glow over the island and the endless sea beyond. At that moment, I understood why Folegandros **stole the hearts of all who visited**.

Day Excursions to Other Cycladic Islands

Beyond these incredible destinations, Milos is the **perfect gateway to even more Cycladic islands**. If you have extra time, consider **hopping on a ferry** and exploring:

- **Serifos** – A rugged, wild island with **untamed beaches and traditional villages**.
- **Ios** – Famous for its **lively nightlife, golden beaches, and charming Chora**.
- **Paros & Antiparos** – A combination of **traditional Cycladic beauty and stunning beaches**, perfect for those seeking both relaxation and adventure.

Final Thoughts: A Journey of Endless Discovery

Every time I set sail from Milos, I felt like I was embarking on **a new adventure**, stepping into **another world waiting to be discovered**. Whether it was the **timeless charm of Kimolos, the untouched beauty of Polyaigos, the elegance of Sifnos, or the cliffside drama of Folegandros**, each island left **a lasting impression on my soul**.

If you're visiting Milos, don't just stay put—**venture beyond, chase the horizon, and uncover the magic of these nearby islands**. The **Aegean is calling**, and I promise, **it will be an adventure you'll never forget**.

Sustainable & Responsible Travel in Milos

Milos is more than just a stunning Greek island—it's a **fragile paradise** shaped by nature and history. From the **moonlike landscapes of Sarakiniko** to the **hidden caves of Kleftiko**, every corner of this island holds a **unique beauty** that deserves our protection. Traveling responsibly isn't just about reducing waste or choosing eco-friendly accommodations; it's about **respecting the land, the people, and the culture that make Milos so special**.

I've always believed that **travel should leave a place better than we found it**. With that mindset, I set out to experience Milos in the most **sustainable, thoughtful, and community-focused way possible**. What I discovered was a deep connection between the island, its people, and the environment—a connection that we, as visitors, have the privilege and responsibility to protect.

Eco-Friendly Accommodations & Tours

One of the easiest ways to make a positive impact in Milos is by choosing **eco-friendly accommodations and sustainable tours**. The island is home to several hotels, guesthouses, and tour operators that prioritize **green practices**, from **solar energy and water conservation** to **zero-waste initiatives**.

Where to Stay Sustainably

When I was looking for a place to stay, I found several **small, locally-owned guest houses** that use **natural materials, recycle water, and minimize plastic waste**. Some even **grow their own food** or use **energy-efficient designs** to keep their carbon footprint low. Staying at one of these places not only helped me travel more responsibly but also **gave me a more authentic experience of island life**.

A few eco-friendly stays to consider:

- **Traditional stone houses** that blend into the landscape and use natural cooling techniques.

- **Solar-powered boutique hotels** with stunning sea views.
- **Family-run guest houses** that serve organic, homegrown produce for breakfast.

Choosing Responsible Tours

Exploring Milos by sea is a must, but I wanted to make sure I did it in a way that didn't harm the delicate marine ecosystem. I found **boat tour operators that use fuel-efficient boats, limit anchor drops to avoid damaging the seabed, and educate visitors on marine conservation**.

Some tours even offer **plastic-free excursions**, providing **reusable water bottles and snacks wrapped in biodegradable packaging**. It was a small change, but it made a big difference in reducing waste on the island.

Supporting Local Communities & Businesses

Traveling responsibly also means ensuring that our money goes directly to **local communities** rather than big international corporations. In Milos, **small businesses,**

artisans, and family-run tavernas are the heart of the island's culture and economy.

Shopping Local & Supporting Artisans

Walking through the charming streets of **Plaka and Adamas**, I came across **small boutiques selling handmade ceramics, jewelry, and traditional Greek textiles**. Each item had a story, and by purchasing from these local artisans, I knew I was helping to **preserve their craft and support their livelihood.**

Dining at Family-Run Tavernas

Rather than opting for big touristy restaurants, I sought out **family-run tavernas,** where the ingredients were **locally sourced and the recipes passed down through generations**. There's nothing like **tasting fresh-caught seafood, homemade cheese,** and **sun-ripened vegetables** while knowing that your meal supports **local farmers and fishers**.

Preserving Milos' Natural Beauty

Milos is a **geological wonder**, filled with **dramatic cliffs, volcanic rock**

formations, and untouched beaches. But as tourism grows, so does the risk of damaging these natural treasures. I made it a point to explore the island in a way that left **no trace behind**.

Respecting Fragile Ecosystems

The **white volcanic cliffs of Sarakiniko**, the **hidden caves of Sykia**, and the **colorful beaches of Firiplaka** are delicate landscapes that can easily be harmed by excessive foot traffic and litter.

To help preserve them, I followed a few simple but important rules:

- **Sticking to marked trails** instead of creating new paths.
- **Avoiding climbing on fraggle rock formations** to prevent erosion.
- **Taking all my trash with me**, even biodegradable items like fruit peels.

Protecting the Marine Environment

The waters around Milos are home to **rare marine life**, including the **Mediterranean monk seal**, one of the world's most endangered species. I made sure that every snorkeling or diving trip I took was with

guides who followed strict conservation rules—like avoiding touching coral, not feeding fish, and keeping a respectful distance from sea creatures.

Responsible Wildlife Encounters

One of the most unforgettable experiences in Milos is witnessing **its incredible wildlife**—but it's crucial that we do so responsibly. I learned that **not all wildlife experiences are ethical**, and some can actually harm the very creatures we admire.

Observing Animals from a Distance

Whether it was **watching seabirds dive into the Aegean** or spotting a **rare monk seal resting on the rocks**, I made sure to keep a **safe and respectful distance**. Approaching too closely can **stress animals and disrupt their natural behaviors**.

Saying No to Exploitative Practices

I also made a point to **avoid any attractions that exploited animals**, such as places that allowed handling of marine life or offered dolphin interactions. Instead, I opted for

ethical eco-tours, where I could learn about wildlife without disturbing it.

Tips for a Greener Vacation

Even small actions can add up to make a big difference in protecting Milos. Here are a few of the habits I adopted during my trip to ensure that I was traveling as sustainably as possible:

1. Pack Light & Smart

I brought a **reusable water bottle, a cloth shopping bag, and a bamboo cutlery set**, which helped me avoid **single-use plastics** throughout my trip.

2. Choose Public Transport or Walk

Instead of renting a car, I explored much of Milos on foot and used **local buses** whenever possible. Walking not only **reduced my carbon footprint** but also gave me a **closer connection to the island's landscapes and people**.

3. Be Water Conscious

Freshwater is limited on Milos, so I took **shorter showers, reused towels, and**

avoided wasting water—a small effort that helps sustain the island's resources.

4. Respect Cultural Traditions

I made sure to **dress modestly when visiting churches, support local festivals, and learn a few basic Greek phrases** as a sign of respect for the local culture.

Final Thoughts: A Commitment to Sustainable Travel

Milos is an island of **raw beauty, rich history, and warm hospitality**, and it's up to us as travelers to ensure that **it remains that way for generations to come**.

I left Milos with **more than just incredible memories**—I left with a **deeper appreciation for responsible travel** and a commitment to making my future trips more sustainable. Whether it's **choosing an eco-friendly stay, supporting local businesses, respecting wildlife, or reducing waste**, every choice we make as travelers matters.

So, when you visit Milos, I encourage you to **travel with intention, with care, and**

with respect. Not only will you have a **more meaningful experience**, but you'll also be part of **protecting this island's magic for the future**.

Milos for Different Travelers

Milos is one of those rare destinations that **has something for everyone**. Whether you're looking for a **romantic escape, a family-friendly adventure, a solo exploration, a budget-friendly getaway, or a luxury retreat**, this island can shape itself to your travel style. I've had the chance to experience Milos from different perspectives, and what I found was that **no matter how you travel, Milos welcomes you with open arms**.

Milos for Couples: Romantic Getaways & Honeymoons

If I had to name the **most romantic Greek island**, Milos would be at the top of my list. There's something undeniably **dreamy** about its **secluded beaches, fiery sunsets, and quiet seaside villages**—the perfect setting for a honeymoon or couples' retreat.

My favorite **romantic experience** in Milos? **Watching the sunset from the Venetian Castle of Plaka**. As the sky turned to **shades of pink, orange, and deep purple**, it felt like time stood still. **Holding hands with a loved one**, surrounded by the **warm Aegean breeze**, was pure magic.

For couples looking for **a private escape**, I recommend booking a **luxury boutique hotel with a sea-view balcony**. If you want something more adventurous, **a boat tour to Kleftiko**—with its hidden caves and crystal-clear waters—feels like discovering your own secret paradise.

Top romantic experiences:

- **A private beach picnic at Tsigrado or Fyriplaka**
- **Candlelit seafood dinner by the water in Pollonia**
- **Couples' sunset sailing tour with champagne**

Whether you prefer **lazy beach days** or **adventurous explorations**, Milos has a way of making every moment feel special for two.

Milos for Families: Kid-Friendly Attractions & Activities

Milos is an amazing island for **families with kids**, thanks to its **calm waters, soft sandy**

beaches, and welcoming locals. I've seen families enjoying the island at their own pace—**building sandcastles at Agia Kyriaki Beach, taking boat trips to hidden caves, or exploring Milos' history in an interactive way**.

One of the best family-friendly spots is **Papafragas Beach**, where **kids can swim safely in a natural rock pool** while parents relax nearby. Another must-do is the **Ancient Theater of Milos**, which brings history to life in a fun and engaging way.

For families who love adventure, a **half-day boat tour to Kleftiko** offers the chance to **snorkel in shallow waters and explore sea caves**—a memory that kids will treasure forever.

Top kid-friendly activities:

- **Visiting the Milos Mining Museum** (perfect for little explorers!)
- **Riding a glass-bottom boat to spot fish and marine life**
- **Hiking to Sarakiniko Beach for a moon-like adventure**

Milos makes traveling with kids **easy and stress-free**, offering **safe beaches, fun**

activities, and a relaxed atmosphere where the whole family can unwind.

Milos for Solo Travelers: Safe & Social Experiences

I'll be honest—Milos is a **dream destination for solo travelers**. There's a sense of **freedom, safety, and adventure** that makes exploring the island alone feel effortless. Whether you want to **meet new people or simply enjoy some peaceful solitude**, Milos gives you both options.

One of the best ways to connect with others is by joining a **boat tour**. These trips tend to have **small, friendly groups**, making it easy to strike up conversations while discovering hidden coves together. I met fellow travelers on a sailing tour to **Kleftiko**, and by the end of the day, we were all sharing stories over fresh seafood in a local taverna.

For solo travelers who love a bit of quiet reflection, **hiking the trails around Plaka** is an amazing way to soak in the island's beauty at your own pace. And the best part? Milos is **one of the safest Greek islands**, so I never felt uneasy exploring on my own, even at night.

Top solo travel experiences:

- **Joining a group boat tour or cooking class to meet other travelers**
- **Enjoying a peaceful morning coffee in Pollonia's charming cafés**
- **Taking self-guided hikes to scenic viewpoints and hidden beaches**

Milos allows solo travelers to **explore freely, meet friendly locals, and embrace the beauty of the island without worry**.

Milos for Budget Travelers: Affordable Stays & Eats

You don't need a luxury budget to experience the magic of Milos. In fact, this island is surprisingly **affordable compared to other Cycladic destinations** like Mykonos or Santorini.

I found that the **best way to save money** was by **staying in family-run guesthouses** and **eating at small local tavernas** where meals are **delicious, generous, and reasonably priced**. In the village of Adamas, I had some of the **best homemade Greek dishes for** under €10—from **stuffed tomatoes to fresh seafood pasta**.

Beaches in Milos are **completely free**, and many of them are accessible by **public transport**, making it easy to explore without renting a car. If you want to visit Kleftiko on a budget, **look for group boat tours instead of private charters**, which cost much less but still offer an amazing experience.

Top budget-friendly tips:

- **Stay in locally-owned guesthouses or budget-friendly hotels**
- **Eat at traditional Greek tavernas where locals go**
- **Use the island's bus system instead of renting a car**

Milos proves that **you don't need to spend a fortune to enjoy paradise**.

Milos for Luxury Travelers: Exclusive & High-End Experiences

For those looking for **a more indulgent escape**, Milos has plenty of **luxurious experiences** that feel both exclusive and intimate. Unlike Mykonos or Santorini, where luxury often means big resorts and crowds, Milos offers **a more private, tailored experience**—which, in my opinion, is even better.

One of the **ultimate luxury experiences** is booking a **private yacht tour** around the island, complete with **champagne, gourmet Greek meals, and stops at hidden beaches only accessible by boat**. Watching the **sunset from a luxury catamaran** while sipping wine? **Pure perfection**.

For accommodation, Milos has a selection of **high-end boutique hotels and private villas**, often with **infinity pools overlooking the Aegean**. Some even offer **spa treatments, personal chefs, and exclusive beach access**.

Top luxury experiences:

- **A private sailing tour with fine dining onboard**
- **Staying in a cave-style luxury suite with panoramic sea views**
- **Indulging in a Greek wine tasting experience with a private sommelier**

If you're seeking **seclusion, comfort, and personalized service**, Milos delivers a **luxury experience that feels intimate and authentic**.

Final Thoughts: Milos is for Everyone

No matter **who you are or how you travel**, Milos has **something special waiting for you**. Whether you're here for **romance, adventure, family fun, solo exploration, budget travel, or high-end luxury**, this island **adapts to your style** and offers an experience that feels uniquely yours.

I came to Milos not knowing what to expect, and I left with **memories that matched every mood and moment of my journey**. And that's the beauty of this island—it welcomes you **just as you are** and gives you an experience that **feels personal, magical, and unforgettable**.

So, how will you experience Milos? However you choose, I promise—it will be **extraordinary**.

Itineraries for Every Type of Traveler

Milos is an island that can be explored at **any pace**—whether you're here for a **short, action-packed escape**, a **balanced mix of adventure and relaxation**, or a **deep dive into its culture, history, and outdoor thrills**. Over my time here, I've realized that **having a well-planned itinerary** makes all the difference. So, whether you have **three days, five days, or a full week**, or if you're drawn to **culture or adrenaline-fueled adventures**, here's how to **make the most of Milos**.

3-Day Itinerary: Quick Highlights of Milos

If you only have three days, don't worry—**you can still experience the essence of Milos**. The key is to **prioritize must-see spots** while leaving some time to unwind.

Day 1: Arrival & Sunset Views

- Arrive in **Adamas**, the island's main port, and check into a **centrally located hotel or guesthouse**.

- Spend the afternoon at **Sarakiniko Beach**, with its **white volcanic cliffs** and **turquoise waters**. It's an **iconic first stop**!
- Head to **Plaka for sunset** at the **Venetian Castle**, with **breathtaking panoramic views**.
- Dine at a traditional **taverna** like **Archontoula**, famous for its **homemade Greek dishes**.

Day 2: Boat Tour & Secluded Beaches

- Take a **half-day boat tour to Kleftiko**, a place **only accessible by sea**, with its **majestic caves and crystal-clear waters**.
- After the tour, enjoy a **relaxing afternoon at Firiplaka Beach**, known for its **colorful cliffs and shallow waters**.
- End the day with **seafood dinner by the water in Pollonia**, a charming fishing village.

Day 3: Culture & Departure

- Visit the **Ancient Theater of Milos** and **the site where the Venus de Milo was discovered**.

- Explore the **Christian Catacombs**, a unique piece of **early Christian history**.
- Have a **final meal at O! Hamos Tavern**, a **farm-to-table restaurant** with delicious local dishes.
- Catch your ferry or flight, **already planning your next visit!**

5-Day Itinerary: Balanced Adventure & Relaxation

With five days, you get the **best of both worlds**—a mix of **sightseeing, adventure, and downtime**.

Day 1-3: Follow the 3-Day Itinerary Above

Day 4: Island Exploration & Hidden Gems

- Rent a **car or ATV** and drive to **Papafragas Beach**, a natural **rock pool perfect for a morning swim**.
- Visit **the Ghost Village of Zefyria**, a mysterious abandoned town with a **rich history**.

- Spend the afternoon at **Kalogries Beach**, a **quiet and untouched paradise**.
- Experience **a sunset sailing cruise**, with stops at **hidden caves and coastal cliffs**.

Day 5: Relaxation & Local Culture

- **Morning at Agia Kyriaki Beach**, a **calm, family-friendly spot** with **golden sands**.
- Explore the **Folklore Museum of Plaka**, which offers a **fascinating glimpse into Milos' past**.
- **End your trip with a luxurious seafood dinner** at a waterfront restaurant in **Mandrakia**.

7-Day Itinerary: Ultimate Milos Experience

A full week in Milos means **no rush, no stress—just pure immersion in everything the island offers**.

Day 1-5: Follow the 5-Day Itinerary Above

Day 6: Day Trip to Kimolos or Polyaigos

- Take a **boat to Kimolos**, Milos' **charming neighboring island**, where you can **wander its whitewashed streets** and **relax on untouched beaches**.
- Alternatively, **visit Polyaigos**, the **largest uninhabited island in Greece**, known for its **stunning blue waters and secluded coves**.

Day 7: Leisure & Final Exploration

- **Spend your last morning at Paleochori Beach**, known for its **thermal waters and vibrant rock formations**.
- Stroll through **Adamas one last time**, picking up **local souvenirs** like handmade ceramics and Greek honey.
- Enjoy a **final meal overlooking the sea**, savoring **one last taste of Milos before heading home**.

Milos for Culture Enthusiasts: A Historical & Artistic Journey

For travelers who love **history, art, and local culture**, Milos is **rich with archaeological wonders and traditional charm**.

Day 1: Ancient Marvels

- Visit the **Archaeological Museum of Milos**, home to **a replica of the Venus de Milo**.
- Explore the **Ancient Theater of Milos**, a beautifully preserved amphitheater overlooking the sea.

Day 2: Religious & Local History

- Tour the **Christian Catacombs**, one of the most significant **early Christian burial sites in Greece**.
- Visit the **Folklore Museum in Plaka**, where you'll get a sense of **Milos' traditional way of life**.

Day 3: Hidden Cultural Gems

- Wander through the **Ghost Village of Zefyria**, a hauntingly beautiful **abandoned town**.
- **Meet local artisans** and shop for **handmade pottery** in Plaka's boutiques.

Milos for Adventure Seekers: Action-Packed Activities

If you crave **excitement and outdoor challenges**, Milos is **a paradise for thrill-seekers**.

Day 1: Hiking & Climbing

- Start with **a morning hike to Profitis Ilias**, the highest peak in Milos, for **unbelievable views**.
- Try **rock climbing at Sarakiniko,** where the **volcanic cliffs make for a dramatic climb**.

Day 2: Water Adventures

- **Go scuba diving** to explore the **underwater caves and shipwrecks**.
- **Kayak along the coastline**, discovering **hidden sea caves and rock formations**.

Day 3: Off-Road Adventures

- Rent an **ATV and drive to remote beaches** like **Kipos and Ammoudaraki**.

- Try **horseback riding along the coast**, a unique way to explore Milos' wild beauty.

Final Thoughts: Your Perfect Milos Experience Awaits

No matter **how much time you have** or **what kind of traveler you are**, Milos offers an **unforgettable experience**. Whether you're here for **a quick escape, a relaxed week, a deep cultural journey, or an action-packed adventure**, there's **a perfect itinerary waiting for you**.

When I first visited Milos, I had **no idea how much it had to offer**. But by planning my days wisely, I was able to **experience its beauty, culture, and adventure to the fullest**. I hope these itineraries help you do the same—**because Milos isn't just a place to visit, it's a place to truly experience.**

Essential Travel Tips & Practical Information for Milos

Visiting Milos is an **exciting, enriching, and unforgettable experience**, but a little planning can go a long way in making your trip as smooth and enjoyable as possible. Whether it's understanding **local customs, knowing how to stay connected, or handling money matters**, I've gathered **all the essential travel tips** you'll need. Think of this as your go-to guide for **a stress-free Milos adventure!**

Safety Tips & Emergency Contacts

Milos is an **incredibly safe island**, with a welcoming community and low crime rates. However, like anywhere in the world, it's always wise to stay aware of your surroundings.

General Safety Tips:

- **Watch Your Step** – Many of Milos' attractions, like Sarakiniko and Kleftiko, have rugged terrain. Wear **sturdy shoes** when exploring.

- **Beach Safety** – Some beaches, such as Tsigrado, require **steep climbs** to access. Always assess if you're comfortable with the descent before attempting.
- **Driving Caution** – Many roads in Milos are **unpaved and narrow**. Drive slowly, especially in rental cars or ATVs.
- **Stay Hydrated** – The **Greek sun is strong**, especially in summer. Carry a bottle of water, wear sunscreen, and avoid hiking during peak heat hours.
- **Swimming Awareness** – While Milos' waters are generally calm, some areas have strong currents. Always swim in designated spots and check local conditions.

Emergency Contacts in Milos:

- **Emergency Services (Police, Fire, Ambulance):** 112
- **Milos Police Station:** +30 22870 21204
- **Milos Health Center (Public Medical Facility):** +30 22870 22700

- **Pharmacies:** Available in Adamas & Plaka, open Mon-Sat (some close midday)
- **Tourist Information:** Available at the port of Adamas

While emergencies are rare, **knowing these numbers can give you peace of mind** during your trip.

Greek Customs & Etiquette

The Greek people are **warm, welcoming, and deeply rooted in tradition**. While tourists are embraced with open arms, showing **respect for local customs** will make your experience even richer.

Key Greek Etiquette Tips:

- **A Simple 'Kalimera' Goes a Long Way** – Saying "Kalimera" (**Good morning**) when greeting locals shows friendliness and respect.
- **Tipping Culture** – Not always expected, but appreciated. At restaurants, **round up the bill** or leave a 5-10% tip for good service.

- **Church Visits** – If visiting a church or monastery, wear **modest clothing** (shoulders and knees covered).
- **Hospitality is Sacred** – If a local offers you something, it's a **sign of generosity**. Even if you don't want it, a polite "Efharisto" (**Thank you**) is appreciated.
- **Dinner is Late** – Greeks dine late, often around **8-10 PM**. Don't be surprised if restaurants are empty before then!
- **Ouzo Etiquette** – If offered a shot of ouzo (an anise-flavored spirit), it's polite to **raise your glass and say "Yamas!"** (Cheers!) before drinking.

Respecting these small customs will **enhance your interactions** with locals and make your trip **even more authentic**.

Useful Greek Phrases for Travelers

While English is **widely spoken** in Milos, learning **a few Greek words** can make a big difference. Locals **appreciate the effort**, and it often leads to **warmer interactions**.

Essential Greek Phrases:

- Hello – Γειά σου (Yia sou)
- Good morning – Καλημέρα (Kalimera)
- Good evening – Καλησπέρα (Kalispera)
- Please – Παρακαλώ (Parakalo)
- Thank you – Ευχαριστώ (Efharisto)
- Excuse me / Sorry – Συγγνώμη (Signomi)
- How much does this cost? – Πόσο κοστίζει αυτό; (Poso kostizi afto?)
- Where is...? – Πού είναι...; (Pou ine...?)
- Do you speak English? – Μιλάτε Αγγλικά; (Milate Anglika?)

Even just **attempting** a few Greek words will **win you smiles** and **better service** from locals.

Currency, ATMs & Payment Options

Milos, like the rest of Greece, uses the **Euro (€)**. While credit and debit cards are accepted in most places, it's always good to **carry some cash**, especially in smaller villages.

Money Tips for Milos:

- **ATMs** – Available in Adamas, Plaka, and Pollonia. However, they can **run out of cash** in peak summer months, so withdraw early.
- **Credit Cards** – Widely accepted in restaurants, hotels, and larger stores. However, some small tavernas or beach bars may be **cash only**.
- **Tipping** – Not obligatory, but rounding up the bill or leaving small change is a good practice.
- **Exchange Rates** – If exchanging money, do so **before arriving in Milos**, as there are limited exchange services on the island.
- **Contactless Payment** – Apple Pay and Google Pay are becoming more common but don't rely on them everywhere.

Being **prepared with both cash and cards** ensures you **won't be caught off guard** when paying for meals, transportation, or shopping.

Internet, SIM Cards & Staying Connected

Staying connected in Milos is **easier than ever**, but having **the right setup** can make all the difference, especially if you need **navigation, communication, or travel updates**.

Internet & Wi-Fi in Milos:

- **Wi-Fi** – Available in most hotels, cafes, and restaurants. However, speeds can vary, especially in **remote areas**.
- **Mobile Data** – Reliable, but coverage may be weak in **secluded beaches or caves**.

Best SIM Cards for Travelers:

If you need **consistent internet access**, consider **getting a local SIM card** upon arrival in Greece. The best options are:

1. **COSMOTE** – Best coverage and fastest speeds (€10-€20 for prepaid data plans).
2. **Vodafone Greece** – Good coverage with affordable tourist SIM options.
3. **WIND** – Budget-friendly, but with **slightly weaker coverage** in remote areas.

If you don't want a local SIM, **international eSIM services** like **Airalo** or **Holafly** are great for short trips.

Power & Plugs:

- **Greece uses Type C and Type F plugs** (European standard).
- **Voltage: 230V** – If traveling from the U.S. or U.K., check if you need a voltage converter for certain devices.

Final Thoughts: Stress-Free Travel in Milos

With these practical tips in mind, you're now **fully prepared** for a **smooth, enjoyable, and stress-free** trip to Milos. Whether it's **staying safe, managing your budget, or communicating with locals**, a little preparation goes a long way.

Milos is **welcoming, breathtaking, and easy to explore,** and by following these essential tips, you can focus on what truly matters—**soaking in the beauty, culture, and unforgettable experiences this island has to offer.**

Final Thoughts & Conclusion

As I reflect on my time in Milos, I can't help but feel a deep sense of **gratitude and wonder**. This island, with its rugged landscapes, crystal-clear waters, and rich cultural heritage, has left an **indelible mark on my heart**—and I know it will do the same for you. There's something about Milos that **lingers in the soul**, something that beckons you to return even before you've left.

If you're searching for a destination that **combines natural beauty, history, adventure, and authenticity**, Milos should be at the very top of your travel list. But Milos isn't just a place you visit—it's an **experience, a feeling, a connection**. It's the warmth of the locals, the taste of freshly grilled octopus by the sea, the golden sunsets that paint the sky over Sarakiniko. It's the kind of place that reminds you why you fell in love with travel in the first place.

Let me share with you the **reasons why Milos is truly special**, and why, once you've set foot on this Cycladic gem, **you'll never want to leave**.

Why Milos Should Be on Your Travel List

Greece is blessed with over **200 inhabited islands**, each with its own charm and personality. But Milos? Milos is different. It has a way of **taking your breath away at every turn**.

First, there's the **raw, untamed beauty**. Unlike some of the more polished and tourist-heavy islands, Milos remains **authentic and unspoiled**. From the white lunar landscapes of Sarakiniko to the hidden sea caves of Kleftiko, the island's natural wonders look like something out of a dream.

Then, there's the **rich history and culture**. The **Venus de Milo**, one of the most famous sculptures in the world, was unearthed right here. The **ancient catacombs**, the ruins of Phylakopi, and the hilltop villages whisper stories of civilizations past. Every cobblestone street, every old fishing boat, every blue-domed church adds another layer to the island's deep **cultural fabric**.

And of course, let's not forget the **food**. Milos is a **paradise for food lovers**, offering some of the freshest seafood and most flavorful

Greek dishes you'll ever taste. Whether it's a plate of **ladenia (Milos' take on pizza)**, a serving of **grilled sea bass**, or a sweet bite of **karpouzopita (watermelon pie)**, every meal feels like a **celebration of life itself**.

But perhaps the best reason to visit Milos is **the feeling it gives you**. It's the peace of watching the waves roll in at a secluded beach, the thrill of discovering a hidden cove, the joy of sharing a meal with new friends. It's a place that makes you **slow down, breathe, and truly appreciate the moment**.

What Makes Milos Special Compared to Other Greek Islands?

Every Greek island has its own personality, but Milos stands apart in so many ways.

Unlike Santorini, which dazzles with its famous caldera, or Mykonos, known for its **cosmopolitan nightlife**, Milos is a place of **undiscovered treasures**. It has all the beauty of the Cyclades but without the overwhelming crowds. It's a place where you can find yourself **completely alone on a secluded beach**, where you can hike to ancient ruins without another tourist in sight.

The coastline of Milos is another thing that sets it apart. With **over 75 beaches**, each with its own character, Milos **boasts the most diverse and stunning shores in all of Greece**. From the **moon-like terrain of Sarakiniko** to the **turquoise waters of Tsigrado**, the **colorful cliffs of Fyriplaka**, and the **fishermen's houses of Klima**, no two spots are alike.

And then, there's the **sense of community**. The locals of Milos are **genuinely welcoming**, always ready to share a story, recommend a hidden taverna, or teach you a word of Greek. Unlike the fast-paced tourism of other islands, here, you **feel like a guest rather than a visitor**.

Milos is **not just a place to check off a list**—it's a destination that invites you to **linger, explore, and fall in love**.

Key Takeaways for an Amazing Trip

If you're planning your adventure to Milos, here are a few things to keep in mind to make your trip **truly unforgettable**:

- **Embrace the Adventure** – Milos rewards those who explore. Some of the best spots require a little effort—whether it's climbing down a rope to reach Tsigrado Beach or taking a boat to hidden sea caves. **Say yes to the adventure.**
- **Slow Down & Savor the Moment** – Don't rush from place to place. Instead, take your time, watch a sunset in Plaka, enjoy a long seaside lunch, and let the island's rhythm guide you.
- **Connect with the Locals** – Whether it's chatting with a fisherman in Mandrakia or learning about traditional cheese-making in a small village, **the people of Milos are what make it so special**.
- **Respect the Island** – Milos is stunningly beautiful, and it's up to us as travelers to keep it that way. Avoid single-use plastics, stick to marked trails, and leave no trace behind.
- **Visit Beyond Summer** – While summer is beautiful, visiting in spring or early autumn means **fewer crowds, cooler weather, and an even more peaceful experience**.

Encouragement to Explore Responsibly

Traveling is a privilege, and with that comes the **responsibility to protect the places we visit**. Milos is a natural wonder, with **fragile ecosystems, historical sites, and a way of life that should be preserved**. By traveling responsibly—**supporting local businesses, respecting wildlife, and minimizing our environmental impact**—we ensure that Milos stays as magical for future generations as it is today.

Take only photos, leave only footprints, and **immerse yourself in the culture rather than just passing through**.

Farewell & Inspiration for Future Travels

As my time in Milos comes to an end, I find myself already **dreaming of my next visit**. There are still beaches to discover, flavors to savor, and moments to experience. But that's the magic of Milos—it never truly leaves you.

I hope that when you visit, you allow yourself to **fully embrace the island's beauty, its history, its people, and its energy**. Let

Milos **surprise you, move you, and change you**. Travel not just with your eyes, but with your heart.

And when you do visit, I'd love to hear your story. What was your favorite beach? What local dish stole your heart? What hidden gem did you uncover? Because that's the beauty of travel—it's a story that never really ends.

So pack your bags, **follow the call of adventure**, and let Milos be the next chapter in your journey. **I promise, it will be unforgettable.**

Made in the USA
Columbia, SC
13 June 2025